In the Picture With

Vincent van Gogh

By Iain Zaczek

WAYLAND

Published in paperback in 2016 by Wayland

Copyright © 2014 Brown Bear Books Ltd.

Wayland, an imprint of Hachette Children's Group
Part of Hodder & Stoughton
Carmelite House
50 Victoria Embankment
London EC4Y 0DZ

Wayland Australia
Level 17/207 Kent Street
Sydney, NSW 2000

All Rights Reserved.

Brown Bear Books Ltd.
First Floor
9–17 St. Albans Place
London
N1 0NX

Author: Iain Zaczek
Managing Editor: Tim Cooke
Designer and artwork: Supriya Sahai
Picture Manager: Sophie Mortimer
Design Manager: Keith Davis
Editorial director: Lindsey Lowe
Children's publisher: Anne O'Daly

ISBN–13: 978 1 5263 0005 8

Printed in Malaysia

10 9 8 7 6 5 4 3 2 1

An Hachette UK company
www.hachette.co.uk
www.hachettechildrens.co.uk

Contents

Life story

Vincent van Gogh is one of the most famous painters in the world. But he did not become an artist until he was 27.

Vincent van Gogh was born in a small village in the Netherlands. He had one brother and three sisters. His father was a Protestant pastor. Vincent was very close to his brother Theo. When they were apart they wrote to each other every week. When Vincent was 16 he got his first job working for a firm that sold paintings. Vincent wasn't much of a businessman but he loved art. He was also good at languages. In 1873 the firm sent him to work in London, England.

Birth name: **Vincent Willem van Gogh**

Born: **30 March, 1853, Zundert, Netherlands**

Died: **29 July, 1890, Auvers-sur-Oise, France**

Nationality: **Dutch**

Field: **Painting, drawing**

Movement: **Post-Impressionism**

Influenced by: **Jean-François Millet, Rembrandt van Rijn, Eugène Delacroix, Impressionism, Ukiyo-e**

Self-portrait with Straw Hat, Paris, Winter 1887

EARLY YEARS Vincent was born in the village of Zundert in the southern Netherlands. This photograph of Zundert was taken in 1902.

An artist's life

Vincent enjoyed life in a big city. He visited art galleries and museums. He even bought a top hat, writing home that everyone in London had one. The job also took him to Paris. But later he lost interest in his work and the firm told him to leave.

Famous Paintings:

* **Sunflowers** 1888
* **The Sower** 1888
* **The Night Café** 1888
* **Irises** 1889
* **Starry Night** 1889

After this, Vincent worked for a while as a teacher and as a preacher. In 1880, at the age of 27, he decided to become an artist. He taught himself how to draw and paint by copying other artists and by reading books.

'I dream of painting and then I paint my dreams.'

While Vincent was learning to paint, his life was difficult. He quarrelled with his father and moved to The Hague. He fell in love there, but his family did not approve of his girlfriend. During this difficult time, however, Theo supported his brother. He sent Vincent money and letters, encouraging him to keep painting.

Key Places

Zundert, Netherlands

London, England

The Hague, Netherlands

Paris, France

Arles, France

Auvers-sur-Oise, France

Vincent eventually moved back in with his parents and painted his first important picture, *The Potato Eaters*. Then in March 1886 he moved to Paris, where Theo was working as an art dealer. Vincent never went home to the Netherlands again.

Theo van Gogh

Vincent's younger brother, Theo, was his closest friend and his greatest supporter. The pair wrote to each other all the time. Vincent wrote to Theo about his paintings. His letters are the main way we know today about how he thought about art.

Theo became an important art dealer in Paris. He got his employers to sell works by new Impressionist painters, such as Claude Monet and Edgar Degas.

PARIS Building of the Eiffel Tower began in 1887, while Vincent was living in the city. It was opened two years later, when he was in Arles.

Life in France

Paris was the centre of the art world, but Vincent fell out with other artists because of his sharp tongue and bad temper. In February 1888 he moved to Arles in the south of France. The locals thought he was a tramp or a lunatic, but soon he settled in and made friends.

'If you hear a voice within you say "you cannot paint", then by all means paint and that voice will be silenced.'

CAFÉ IN ARLES
Arles was a busy town. Vincent spent a lot of his time relaxing with his friends in the town's many cafés and bars.

Self portrait with Yellow Christ, 1890, by Paul Gauguin

Paul Gauguin

Vincent's friend, Paul Gauguin, experimented with unrealistic colour. One example was "Self-Portrait with Yellow Christ." After he left Arles, he never saw Van Gogh again, but the two men continued to write to each other.

Difficult times

Vincent wanted to found an artists' colony. He invited the painter Paul Gauguin to join him. Although the two men got along reasonably well, they were very different. After a few months they quarrelled. Vincent threatened Gauguin with a razor, then cut off part of his own ear. It was the first sign of his mental illness.

I did not have to go out of my way very much in order to try to express sadness and extreme loneliness.

Vincent began to see things that weren't there. For 12 months he was a patient in an asylum (hospital) for the mentally sick. When he left hospital in May 1890 he moved again. He settled in Auvers-sur-Oise, a village north of Paris. There he was close to his brother Theo. A doctor who knew many painters kept an eye on him.

SOUTH OF FRANCE
Vincent loved the light of southern France and the bright colours of plants like lavender and sunflowers.

Vincent was happy — until his illness returned. He felt desperate that he would never be cured. On 27 July, 1890, he shot himself. He died two days later, with Theo at his side. Vincent was 37. He had only been an artist for 10 years, but had painted nearly 900 paintings.

'In a picture I want to say something comforting.'

SUNFLOWERS IN ARLES
There were fields of sunflowers near Arles. The large yellow flowers made Vincent cheerful.

How van Gogh painted

Vincent painted in several styles. When he moved to Paris, he was affected by a group of artists known as the Impressionists.

The Impressionists used new ways to try to paint things as they really looked. Vincent also spent time with Paul Gauguin and other artists who were experimenting with unusual painting styles.

Japanese Prints

Japanese art was very popular in Paris. Vincent admired the way artists like Hokusai used flat colours and simple shapes. This picture by Hokusai shows a man returning home after gathering rushes.

IMPASTO Vincent used thick strokes of paint that were built up in uneven layers.

SWIRLY LINES In Vincent's paintings, the sky is full of lines, suggesting energy.

A personal style

The influence of other artists helped Vincent develop his own style of painting. Like the Impressionists, he painted from real life, rather than from his imagination.

Many features of his style were inspired by Japanese prints. He used bright colours that were not like the ones found in nature. He used simple shapes and did not try to make a scene look 3-D.

Vincent painted very thickly so that the paint stood out from the canvas. This technique is called impasto. In his last paintings, Vincent used swirling lines that seem like ripples of energy.

Important Impressionists

Edouard Manet

Claude Monet

Camille Pissarro

Pierre-Auguste Renoir

Mary Cassatt

Berthe Morisot

Alfred Sisley

The Potato Eaters

This was Vincent's first important picture. He painted it in 1885, while he was living in Nuenen in the Netherlands.

Vincent was busy learning to paint well. This picture was inspired by his hero, the French artist Jean-François Millet. Millet had painted peasants at work. Van Gogh wanted to show poor farmers eating their meal. He used models whose faces were coarse and ugly. He told Theo that he wanted the rich people who saw his painting to think about poor people's lives.

VAN GOGH'S
Palette of the picture

This painting has the shape of a cross. It shows that the peasants are religious.

The peasants are eating together but they all seem to be quiet and alone.

Vincent enjoyed painting the effects of the lamplight reflected in this peasant's cheeks.

In the Frame

🖊 The original painting of *The Potato Eaters* is 82 cm (32.3 inches) tall and 114 cm (44.9 inches) wide.

🖊 Vincent painted two versions of this picture. He also made a print of it.

🖊 It was Vincent's favourite among his early works.

Vincent used gloomy colours in the painting. They are like the colours of the earth and the land.

Sunflowers

Vincent painted lots of pictures of sunflowers. The flowers grew around Arles, where he first painted them in summer 1888.

Vincent had rented a new house. He was looking forward to the arrival of his friend, the painter Paul Gauguin. Vincent wanted the sunflower pictures to decorate his friend's bedroom. He hoped to paint twelve pictures, but only painted four. Later, he made more versions of the four paintings.

Sunflowers grew wild around Arles. Many artists used them as symbols of happiness and friendship.

> The whole thing will be a symphony of yellow and brown.

In the Frame

🌻 The original painting of *Sunflowers* is 92.1 cm (36.2 inches) tall and 73 cm (28.7 inches) wide.

🌻 There are many versions. This one is in the National Gallery, London.

Vincent had to paint quickly, because the flowers faded within hours of being picked.

VAN GOGH'S

Palette of the picture

Vincent often applied his paint very thickly. The seed heads are painted with thick dabs of paint.

Most artists painted objects with no outlines. Inspired by Japanese art, Vincent did the opposite.

Vincent often did not sign his paintings. Here his signature is on the vase, as if it belongs to the potter.

Portrait of Père Tanguy

Vincent loved to paint portraits. This one shows his friend Julien 'Père' Tanguy. Vincent painted this picture in 1887.

Tanguy sold art supplies in Paris. He was so kind to the artists that they called him Père, or 'father.' If an artist was poor, Tanguy let him have supplies in return for a picture. He built up a collection of paintings by young artists. Going to Tanguy's shop was like visiting an art gallery of the best artists in Paris. Vincent was influenced by the paintings he saw there.

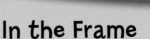

The background includes one of Vincent's own paintings, which he had given to his brother.

This is not a realistic view of Tanguy's gallery. The prints are too large compared with the man.

VAN GOGH'S

Palette of the picture

In the Frame

🌷 The original painting *Portrait of Père Tanguy* is 92 cm (36.2 inches) tall and 75 cm (29.5 inches) wide.

🌷 Vincent painted three versions of the picture. This is the second version.

The background shows some of the Japanese prints Tanguy sold.

This figure almost seems to touch Tanguy's arm. The picture's lack of depth shows the influence of Japanese art.

The Artist's Bedroom in Arles

Van Gogh painted this picture of his bedroom in Arles, southern France, in October 1888. This was a happy time in his life.

Vincent was looking forward to starting an artists' colony in Arles with the painter Paul Gauguin. His painting of his bedroom was cheerful and relaxing. He wanted it to make people think about sleeping or resting. He wrote to Theo that he wanted the large flat colour areas to look a bit like a Japanese print.

I liked to draw solid outlines for most objects.

As in a Japanese print the objects in the picture don have any shadows.

The paintings on the wall changed in the three different versions of the painting.

In the Frame

🍂 The original painting *Bedroom in Arles* is 72 cm (28.3 inches) tall and 90 cm (35.4 inches) wide.

🍂 The room was in the corner of a hotel, and the walls were at a strange angle.

🍂 Vincent painted three versions of this picture.

The objects on the wall are arranged in pairs. They look neat and tidy.

VAN GOGH'S

Palette of the picture

The bed looks sturdy, warm and comfortable. The splash of red on the bed is the strongest colour in the picture.

The Night Café

When he arrived in Arles, Vincent rented a room above a café. In September 1888 he stayed up three nights in a row to paint how the café appeared late at night.

Vincent was experimenting with painting at night. He said that he wanted to use bright colours to suggest 'terrible passions'. He knew that the colours were not realistic, but he thought they showed strong emotion. Although the scene is gloomy, and some customers seem to be asleep, the café still seems lively.

In the Frame

🖌 The original painting of *The Night Café* is 72.4 cm (28.5 inches) tall and 92.1 cm (36.3 inches) wide.

🖌 Van Gogh gave the picture to the café owner in place of the money he owed him.

The floor and billiard table seem to slope towards the viewer, creating an unreal effect.

The white coat of the café owner looks yellow in the artificial light.

Vincent painted huge gas lamps. The short lines suggest the light coming out of the lamps.

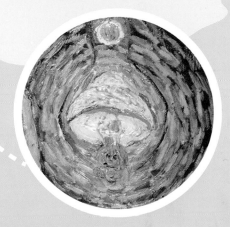

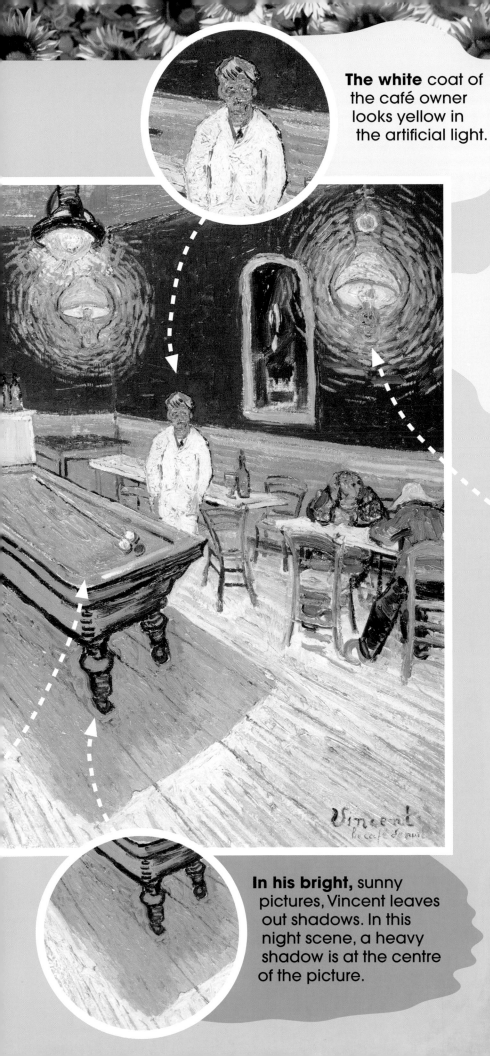

Vincent
le café de nuit

VAN GOGH'S

Palette of the picture

In his bright, sunny pictures, Vincent leaves out shadows. In this night scene, a heavy shadow is at the centre of the picture.

Starry Night

Vincent painted this famous picture when he was in hospital in June 1889. He was not well, and kept having dark and crazy thoughts.

This painting shows the view from Vincent's room. He did not paint it from life, however. He painted it from memory during the day. That allowed him to use far more of his imagination than in the pictures he did from life.

In the sky, great swirls of energy join up the stars. It looks as if something has upset the heavens above the quiet town.

In the Frame

The original painting of *Starry Night* is 73.7 cm (29 inches) tall and 92.1 cm (36.25 inches) wide.

The town in the painting is Saint-Rémy-de-Provence, France.

The flame-like cypress tree juts into the swirling sky. Vincent loved to paint cypresses.

Swirls of paint suggest lots of movement and energy in the sky.

Around the moon Vincent combines short, sharp dashes with long, wavy lines to give the impression of moonlight.

VAN GOGH'S

Palette of the picture

In contrast to the swirling sky and tree, the straight lines of the church steeple have a sense of calm and stillness.

Self-Portrait with Bandaged Ear

Vincent painted more than 40 portraits of himself. This one was painted early in 1889. This was one of the worst times of his life.

He had fought with his friend Paul Gauguin. When Vincent pulled out a razor, Gauguin ran away. Vincent was so upset he cut off part of his own ear. This was the first time it became clear that Vincent had a mental illness. He spent two weeks in hospital to recover from his injury.

In most of his portraits Vincent gazes directly at the viewer. Here, he is lost in his own thoughts.

The bandage covers the wound Vincent made when he cut his ear.

VAN GOGH'S
Palette of the picture

In the Frame

🖌 The original painting of *Self-Portrait with Bandaged Ear* is 60 cm (23.6 inches) tall and 49 cm (19.3 inches) wide.

🖌 Vincent may have painted the portrait to show everyone that he had recovered from his illness.

A Japanese print on the wall is a reminder of Vincent's dream of starting an artists' colony with Gauguin.

I painted more than 40 portraits of myself!

Vincent is wearing a coat and hat indoors. This suggests he is still unwell.

What came next?

Vincent influenced many later artists. He was especially important to two groups of painters.

In the first decade of the 20th century a group of artists in France became known as the Fauves. The word 'fauves' means 'wild beasts'. They got this name because they did not follow any artistic rules. Like Vincent, they did not try to paint how things really looked. They used bright, unnatural colours.

Famous Fauves

- Henri Matisse
- André Derain
- Georges Rouault
- Maurice de Vlaminck
- Raoul Dufy

MACKE stretches shapes and blurs their edges to show a mood.

August Macke
Girls Under Trees, 1914

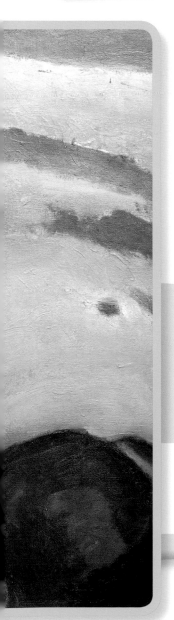

EXPRESSIONIST
Franz Marc uses brighter colours than we would see in reality.

Franz Marc
Horse in a Landscape, 1910

Around the same time, Expressionism emerged in Germany. The Expressionists were inspired by the way that Vincent changed shapes to show a mood or an idea. They started to use bright colours and stretched shapes, like Vincent's stars in *Starry Night*.

The Expressionists

- Edvard Munch
- Oscar Kokoschka
- Franz Marc
- August Macke
- Marc Chagall

How to paint like van Gogh

Vincent had a very individual style. You can try copying one of his paintings, but you can also have fun making your very own van Gogh.

WHAT YOU'LL NEED:

- a mirror (for a self portrait)
- thick white paper or card
- a pencil
- brushes
- acrylic paints

1.

If you want to try a self portrait, you'll need a mirror.

2.

Use a pencil to lightly sketch the outline of your face. Vincent used simple shapes, so don't include too much detail. If part of your face seems more important than others, you could make it a little bigger.

3.

Colour in the background. Vincent used flat background colours, as in *Sunflowers*.

4.

Now draw a thick black outline around some areas. Or try another of Vincent's tricks. Paint short lines of colour around the face to give a sense of movement and energy.

5.

Fill in the colour on your face. Use bold colours—remember they don't have to be realistic. Van Gogh used short brushstrokes to build up thick layers of oil paint. You can get the same effect with acrylic paints. Work on different parts of the painting in turn, so that each patch has a chance to dry a little before you add the next colour.

Timeline

- **1853:** Born in Zundert, in the Netherlands.

- **1869:** Gets a job in an art gallery.

- **1873:** Works in London.

- **1875:** Goes to work in Paris.

- **1876:** Works as a preacher in Belgium.

- **1880:** Starts to study painting.

- **1886:** Moves to Paris, where he meets the Impressionists.

- **1888:** Moves to Arles. Becomes ill and falls out with Paul Gauguin.

- **1889:** Spends a year in the hospital.

- **1890:** Moves to Auvers-sur-Oise to recover. When his sickness returns, he takes his own life.

Glossary

canvas: A kind of thick fabric that is used as a painting surface for oil paints.

colony: A group of similar people who all live in the same place.

Expressionist: One of a group of artists who tried to show emotion and meaning rather than reality.

impasto: A style of painting in which paint is applied so thickly that it shows the marks of the brush or palette knife.

Impressionist: One of a group of artists who tried to show objects as they appeared at a first glance.

palette: The range of colours an artist uses in a particular painting or group of paintings.

perspective: A technique used in painting to make it seem as if the scene being depicted has depth.

print: A picture that is meant to be reproduced, or copied, many times.

symbol: Something visible that stands for something that is invisible or is a sign of something you can't see.

Further information

BOOKS

Anholt, Laurence. *Van Gogh and the Sunflowers* (Anholt's Artists). Barron's Educational, 2007.

Bodden, Valerie. *Van Gogh* (Xtraordinary Artists). Creative Education, 2008.

Holt, Fiona. *Junior Vincent Van Gogh* (Smart Reads for Kids). CreateSpace, 2013.

Spence, David. *Van Gogh* (Great Artists and their World). Newforest Press, 2010.

Tanner, Max. *What's So Great About Van Gogh?* CreateSpace, 2013.

Vincent Van Gogh Colouring Book. Prestel, 2009.

Wood, Alix. *Vincent Van Gogh* (Artists Through the Ages). Windmill Books, 2013.

WEBSITES

www.vangoghgallery.com
This huge Van Gogh site includes pages of fun facts.

www.ducksters.com/biography/artists/vincent_van_gogh.php
An illustrated biography on the Ducksters website.

www.bbc.co.uk/learningzone/clips/vincent-van-gogh/9079.html
A short BBC Learning Zone video in which an actor plays Van Gogh and explains his work.

makingartfun.com/htm/f-maf-art-library/van-gogh-biography.htm
'Meet Vincent Van Gogh' page from Art Library, with links to projects.

MUSEUMS

You can see Vincent's famous paintings from this book in these museums:

The Potato Eaters
Van Gogh Museum, Amsterdam, Netherlands.

Sunflowers
National Gallery, London, UK.

Portrait of Père Tanguy
Our version of the painting is in a private collection. You can see a later version at the Musée Rodin in Paris, France.

Bedroom in Arles
Van Gogh Museum, Amsterdam, Netherlands.

The Night Café
Yale University Art Gallery, New Haven, CT, USA.

Starry Night
Museum of Modern Art, New York City, USA.

Self-Portrait with Bandaged Ear
The Courtauld Gallery, London, UK.

Publisher's note to educators and parents: Our editors have carefully reviewed these websites to ensure that they are suitable for students. Many websites change frequently, however, and we cannot guarantee that a site's future contents will continue to meet our high standards of quality and educational value. Be advised that students should be closely supervised whenever they access the Internet.

Index